SEX MACHINES

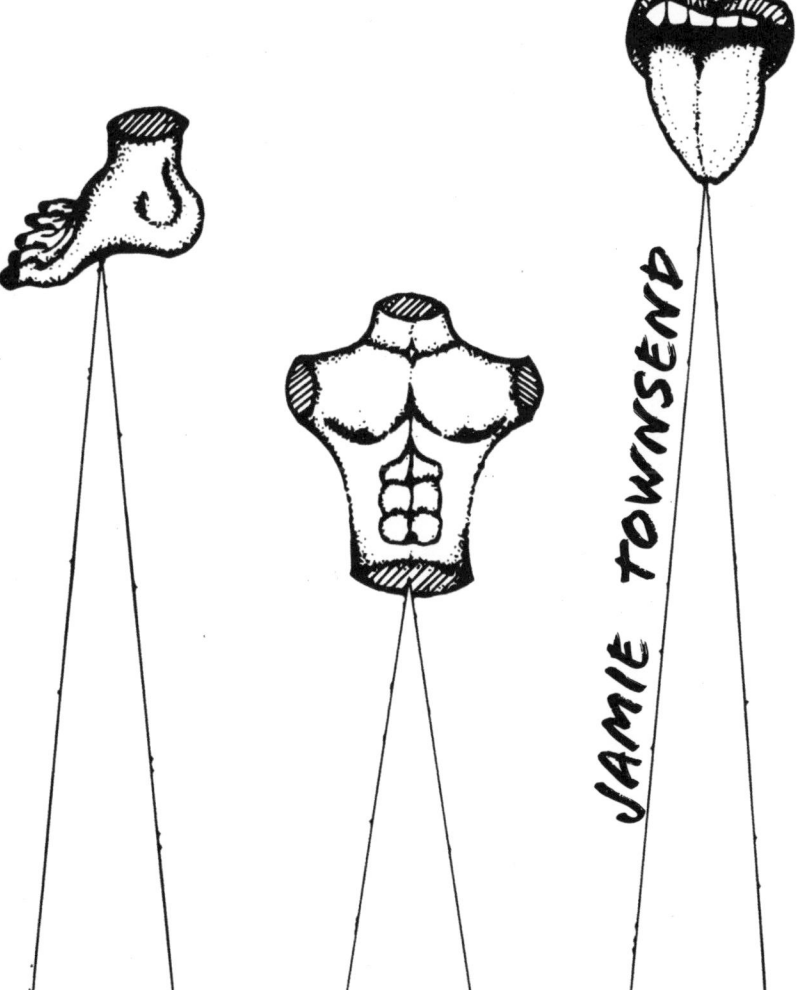

JAMIE TOWNSEND

SEX MACHINES

JAMIE TOWNSEND

speCt!

Editors:
Peter Burghardt
Gillian Olivia Blythe Hamel
Chris Philpot
Robert Andrew Perez
Oakland, CA
spectbooks.com

Cover design by Peter Burghardt and interior layout by speCt!.
Cover is printed using a C&P pilot press. Typefaces used are
Goudy Old Style, Flood Std, and Avenir.

CONTENTS

'A *dish of someone else's amazing burning / figurine*' –kari edwards

PREFACE

Is a hate

Where morning seems

Inevitable

You died we are

Writing our book

In lipstick

ETERNAL PRESENT

Bette writes "Scream Our Tits Off"

Beatriz shaves their pubes for a beard

Alok feels the pressure every day

Genesis caps their teeth in gold

Kate performs Hard Candy

VD reimagines The Magic Flute

Herculine requests that Sara dress them

Anohni punches a ghost

JD opens for Peaches

Aja sings "Level Ya Pussy Up"

Billy plays Hifi on Piano

Justin stars in Mx. America

Leslie is ready to fight

Juliana drips on their rig

kari stretches the life of pie

Candy lives on their deathbed

ANIMAL PRINT

Jessica Jones has a Schiele hanging by her nightstand

Portrait of a portrait artist watching her sleep

It's a heavy cross to bear being tampered with

Disemboweled all angles flushed and distant

Being a sweetness acidic and TBH not very sweet in our mouth

Being labeled a carnivorous flower the sentiment can be reclaimed

A symbol is not genteel it sucks the juices from the living

We're painting the roses red

Roses for vampires, briars, kohl-eyed and wrapped around yr finger

The musk of delicate princess roses marking their bed with thorns

The tenderness, the strength causing a sexual uproar

Blotting the feminine til it blurs into leather

Pink leather at a bachelorette

Ready to crack some plastic cocks together

CRIB IN MY CLOSET

Silk balaclava

Black dahlia on a rose gold Saab

Versailles at Samhain, pentagrams in gold leaf

This dirt is sweet, I want to stuff my mouth

As the allure of failure recedes

I lounge in a misshapen suit

A shape-shifting clown

John Waters with Mike Kelley décor

Love masquerading as clutter

There's blood on the mirror

Medusa on our sneakers

A heat that makes the air feel regal

Dizzy midway through life

On our escalator to nowhere

Mermaid out of water

The concession of a pink burn

On our shoulders

So the misdirection can seem rewarding

Faux fur's warm indifference

The play doesn't care who makes it

In the game of resurrection

Is it enough just to stay alive? Diamonds

Dancing on the head of a diamond

BOUTIQUE

I thought I had escaped my past or lapped

Mondegren couched in sound and intellect

The pricetag of which so bright it burns a hole in my head

'Just visiting, just kidding,' it's a lonely weekend, a lonely feeling

A stretch of retail therapy or medical tourism

It's fall in Soho and I wear a perfect nightgown

Head in the clouds, shuffling through a pile of e-waste

Minimal, aerodynamic, essentially immortal

Like a cruel angel, reclined and slightly nauseous

Losing track of everyone on a train to Newark

But still needing to get the fuck on that plane

Where a mounting anxiety fleshes out the hazy sky

Like a little too high, remembering

The give of thick crepe on grass

I read The Wrestling Party and wait for a happy coincidence

The overwhelming urge to bump into each other

As it's the only way we get a chance to visit

Compliment on a complicated scarf

Concrete jungle feeling like a natural

Indictment of these sartorial autumn trees

Bright jumper, throwback parachute pants

Afraid deep down of being a dick

Or a pink portal printed on a hundred dollar tee

We pose an existential threat to the city

Being young and living on the median strip

In the dim glow of a thousand dreaming ATMs

Not the west coast where manzanitas do all the heavy lifting

Burn to shine, refuse to move

"My neck, my back, my Netflix, and my snacks"

On the edge of a panic attack

I sip a CBD latte and Zoom home

'All this jewelry ain't no use when it's this dark' – Frank Ocean

POPPIES

I can smell chlorine through the photo

Everything but the girl's eden

Sallow tindr pic mouthing a pronoun

Veiling their eyes from I don't know what

My reflection seems so black and white

Smoking gelato in a raspberry beret

It looks like brutalism, I look so flat-footed

The illusion of control slipping from the tips of my fingers

How I became one with the invisible all

Huffing spirals of emerald below

California's state flower dreaming of HD

Not what you think it means

Poison of abundance, soft doom

We drifted off to Bardo Pond

A naptime playlist droning from our phone

Where revolution is waiting for the new moon

Slipping into a peignoir, burning your books

I bought a vintage thong and wondered

How much life is left

THE MYSTERIES OF LOVE

It was cliché like describing a dream

Something singular I couldn't grasp, I wanted to curl up

And undress as the scene escapes me, one night last year

After you fell asleep I took an Ativan, shaved my legs, chest and ass

When I got into bed I jostled you from sleep

We watched Black Mirror, I didn't reveal anything

The quilt became a surrogate lover above my white camisole

A gift I unwrapped in the dark

So quiet I could hear it grow

It felt different it was not the end of things

Only terror which meant we had to deal with the future

That every lost would return again

Inevitable, in this episode the woman runs

From a robotic dog, I think it was a dog

Or maybe a memory of original sin

When I was young and undefined a dog

Chased me into the road it might have been a robot

So singular was its intent but it stuck its tongue out

Like a deer in the headlights I watch MIT robotics videos

On YouTube headless they run at incredible speeds

Nightmare creature staggering over a hill, so singular

I wasn't thinking that moment of being streamlined

Only it felt good not to be a robot and I was afraid

I wanted to tell you, I knew it would come back

To haunt me like there was a transmission in my skin

Lit red marking my location

"Each tiny hair screaming"

It was hard to remove, I missed the picture

Uncanny the screen on top of the blanket

Between us that feeling when you're young

Or maybe also when you're old I'm not sure yet

Your knees form a soft landscape

A valley the light from the screen settles into

Triangulating a moving target we fucked here

I wanted to be closer to the lack, I wanted to lose

A little weight make it easier to slip into the shadow

Where it cracked me open, groomed me a little

Sharing warmth though we didn't understand the source

As it glowed sharp on the soft landscape

That we fit perfectly with it between us

Being followed all the time

It was good to sleep with the window open

LOW HANGING FRUIT

There's a little waterfall in my mind and I'm stuck

In the whirlpool beneath it

We don't want to feel forced to do the right thing

In a situation where we have to chose between

Understanding pleasure and experiencing it

So much conversation fills in the space where I shake

My head and my face becomes a blur and the choice

Seamlessly blurs into fate, bikini briefs

Or cotton boyshorts, the promise of breathability

Feelings of idleness and stimulation

I sleep in a tee with the word bacchanal sprawled across my chest

Count my breaths, exhale more than I take in

St. Dymphna dancing the falling down dance

Anxiously waiting for the dangling sword of god

We're hard and cold down here, trembling beneath her touch

Like when Prince sings "I wanna be your lover

And your mother and your sister" tell me we don't have to choose

Between our mood swings the world lulls into baby talk

Something undefined fits between my skin and the air in this room

I MUFFLE YOUR INNER CHOIR

I try to tie a cherry stem with my tongue and fail miserably

I pull the skin across my teeth and spit out two pits

I look up and worship the moon because it's a shield against my guilt

Most things move on their own

I'm trying to be careful of my xo, my predilection to draw everyone close

When I study the mirror I can't see us

Though I know we're in there

A naked doll smooth as a dolphin

The drug I'm looking for doesn't really exist

I extend my hands, they seem as alien as wings

Cruising across the microscopic surface of a strawberry

As I need to find a place to rest my eyes

I fret about the sins of his father and look over my shoulder

This restlessness, this lack of attention

I suck in my stomach and pull up our skirt

"I'm like Icarus whose wings melted before he could fuck the sun"

The only time I pray is when I'm wasting our time

ENERGY VAMPIRE

I'm studying how to dress well, our louche anxiety

Stripping from it what I can

'without your neck to kiss, I was thrown to the night'

I read this like sucking blood or quoting Celine Dion

All these young dudes are trying to tug at my heartstrings

While they spread their legs I stiffen into

White columns of a mausoleum our love mistakes for authenticity

Violence is full of the shape our art steps into

Inadequate space I'm trying to reclaim as legion swirls through

The night a forest tugging at our loins

And the blush feels resonant, like a drum head rasped

With innumerable waves embracing and pulling us away

To a place where wriggling nests of tentacles greet us with hunger

An army not the orgy I imagined

"My dreams hold death in diamond drag" –Lyn Hejinian

CLONE WAR

I breathe in your vacuum, and shrink under pressure

I swallow a condom full of antimatter

I use your middle finger as my placeholder

Wipe your dust off my shoulder and into the wind

I press an endless pleat into your jeans

I scrubbed the bathroom floor so you could lick your plate clean

After a fitful sleep I split the knees of my jeans scrubbing the sheets

I tilt my head forward so exhaustion seems noir

Every red light an omen

"You fear my limitless emotions"

I remember when the drugs were difficult

I choke on our nostalgia

My blouse is open, I rip your flannel into ribbons

I will be your shadow behind a sheet

Our bathtub streaked in blood

The only one who can see what's really inside

You binge American Horror Story

I scrape your plate over the hole in the center of our galaxy

You wanted to coerce my senses, I wanted to float in your eye

I wore a Nudie suit and felt desolate, vast and sparkling

I contorted myself and clipped my wings

I cling to your crumbling temple columns

I wipe the dust off a book of other worlds previously unseen

I cling to contradictory impulses

Your complaints drowned out by my heartbeat

My anxious heart mocking your retirement

I lay out your clothes every night before

I fall asleep in the bed that we make

KIDDIE POOL

Extolling the virtues of theft

Meaning makes less in a week than

Your masterpiece is for smashing

Porcelain pink panther

Punching a canvas til it's tender

We listened to ArtPop and dream what could've been

Genderqueer porn like *sexy backyard BBQ*

A banana is a bandana is sometimes not

An orange pool toy glowing

In our brain barely there tiger print bandeau

I wanted something lasting I woke up

With a black and blue eye

No gods no masters, I can't see where we end

No need for a period, finish them

LOVE MACHINES

A luminous sword in the hand of an archangel

Purrs with the lightest touch

Their coat rough in its elegance, waxen and accent particolored

Visions descend to replace the salt of the earth

Water gives of air, fire of fire, powder and air draws in

The clouds really a shitty concealer, really just a honey trap

Hanging there we're moths to a neon sign

Cold energy gathering round the makeup mirror

Redolent in the allure of total obliteration

We can live on modest dreams but will starve at their abundance

We blink and it's the boring future

Metallic clouds where we curate our own glimmer

Of understanding which tells us there's a protocol

We need to follow aisle by aisle under fluorescence the scent

That spins us backward where we can smell like a campfire

Or dancing with an DIY perfumer

Straight until the sun goes down

But for the time being I am in the center of everything that screams and teems —Clarice Lispector

WHITE RABBIT

for Julian Brolaski

"We're painting the roses red"

In HD there's a ripeness to the blood

I speak for candida

we read Aqua Viva tipsy

'Yes this is life seen by life'

FROM OUR HEART TO YOURS

At first I was called a character

He was gay and confused at the expectations

Too young to die when he was younger and working out

A future Health Ledger would embellish these polaroids with nail polish

Now I'm sort of framing his golden reflection like in a pool

Of milk and he became something beautiful like an illusion of

Crawling inside my skin to release the tension of being alone

Drifting in a rancher's tan and denim beneath the big sky

Where the rings of Uranus chime like the prayer of a saint in a pit

Just swaying as the surface bends then breaks

As we sway, almost distracted, to his liturgy

EYE GUNK

We disappear into every room that has a mirror

As if there really was an other side

Sweet and chemically altered

Turns out this is not a successful intervention

More than a wrinkle in time

As it sinks in, irreducibly complex

The wasted space that recedes behind us

Like an ass gone to seed

Feelings are hard to control with a shaky hand

Love is patient but often unkind in its restraint

Not wanting to seem too eager

Not sucking too hard on the cut

I thought we meant huge, a secret crush

The sky crammed into a bath bomb

Easing ourselves into the glitter

It's hard to control how it spreads

A purple that's thick and pulsing

A fin barely breaking the surface

CARE BEAR

After Charmin Ultra

Irresistibly soft

    And useless

HEY VENUS

Someday I'll be an old man crying to Frankie Avalon

Someday mid aria I'll snap out of this trance

Someday I'll figure out the right dose

Someday I'll eat the placenta

Someday I'll stop bleeding

Someday I'll stop having sex altogether

Someday I'll be swept off my feet

Someday this romper will fit perfectly

Someday I'll be a old woman crying to Dolly Parton

Someday my ass will lose its definition

Someday this cup will overflow

Someday my breasts will swell

Someday my cock will vanish into thin air

Someday bacteria will eat me out

Someday I'll have my cake and eat it too

Someday I'll meet my long lost twin

Someday I'll be Dennis Cooper

Someday I'll be Britt Marling

Someday everyone will be gone

Someday euphoria will win

Someday I'll be a heart knowing its muscle

MALL GOTH

for Ivy Johnson

We share a makeup mirror

That translates each tilt of the head

Possession is a red light unto our feet

Uncertain and full of doubt

In the darkness of the metal club

We bought a shirt spelling out our disillusion

FEAR GOD THE BODY

An anemic rebellion that spins us backwards

Sex makes an offer with eternity that is declined

Fingering the cold tits of bombs

Solar systems pulled like beads on a string

Through a hole in the sun, our flirtation

Mirrored on the most ludicrous scale

No lovers appear to mourn a self-induced cancer

A little eyeliner dot in the shape of a black heart or tear

A sartorial sorrow spilling coins and pentagrams

Feathers, scales, horns

Terrible supplicant walking around in our shadow

Our soul climaxes so deep inside

We maintain a kind of bored composure

We sing and it's the voice of an animal

Mascara mascara mascara

Smoking cloves by the courtyard

Where the memory of winter is fragrant death

Everything here moves listlessly toward collapse

50,000 years in a frozen wasteland

15 minute coffee break

Ashes drifting from Hot Topic like feedback

Like a t-shirt bought in a metal club

'I am the god of fuck'

Drink from my blood

A bored erotics

A nudity slowly pierced by poison arrows

Puissance leaking reverb and aria

Sullen we held onto the weight of it

We went mad at the lack of attention

We read Nerval in bed

Dumb before the enormous, suffering angel of death

The slow crush of a deflating devil

Hanging above the stage

We pray for the hammer of the sun

In the story of the flood

By nature our metaphors are always mixed

Wreckage of a ship flying black sails

Stone circles under burning churches

Misinterpreting the meaning of

'Kissed by a rose on the grave'.

'Rejoice for I am endless in a garter belt and slip, rejoice!' –Trace Peterson

FLESH LIGHT

I write a list poem

A love letter to Tim Dlugos thrust into me

What leaks out is valuable

Clear as fog and soft

If we make a language of representation

Wings and a cock, it's dawn

We speak and get hard

This list points to the inevitable

Forms for pharmaceuticals to unlock

Bodies in poems

Becoming real in my mouth

Not the low-hanging fruit I was craving

Consumptive wishing for a hole

To hide myself in, a crooked garden

New hope it seems reciprocal

We were scrolling thru what you wrote

Toy of the sacred

Steve's slanted clit

The limits of our imagination

Buy a book of poems

A book about writing poems

An audio book narrated by god

A machine to get you off

DIVORCED

I can't recall exactly when we split

Coercing a false confession from the remains of our grief

Growing greater than the sum of its parts

Memory is a fickle thing, alluring when it grips me

Waiting under the bed in the dark parts

I remember finding a phallus in a drawer

At 13 needing to touch something hard, real

And too big to imagine there was a rabbit

Underground in a horror film a giant

Rabbit or swarm of ants, something hidden in a hole

Hard to consider it belonged to someone I'd never met

Our father's roommate away for the weekend

Though I was a guest

I had made myself at home like an invasion

An idea I still don't understand I'm not expected to though

Eventually I discovered that spit is the best lube

Something of my own hard and fixed and hidden in plain sight

I hide our face and forget maybe it's just the makeup

Maybe it was the want of connection then

Before we appeared and the silk that surrounded it

Being unmentionable but not untouchable or should be

An expression hard and wanting

ANTICHRIST

Online my desire is bald

A perfect circle

A harlequin's cheek

A snakeskin bangle

This ancient rite of passage

Living beyond our means

At the last minute we win the bid

Goodbye paycheck

Hello t-shirt

Stretched over a click hole

A spinning circle of death

Keep watching, up next

A cat got into the cream

Just lapping it up

SUGAR & THE MORTUARY ARTS

I.

I would die in your eyes for lack of subtlety

We watch the angelic conversation hover right at the edge of fullness

Unblinking the mirror reveals an endless chain of meaning

In your eyes I won't apologize for it

Our bed is a packet of sweetener, our lover a continent of blood

Sweeter still the fluid which gives us life

Beyond life passed like wind ripping through an ornamental fan

Like a night filled with the engine of our suffering

Or lust equal parts baleful and anointed

Drained and reanimated in a gilded palace of sin

We blush and it's only a little trick of the light

II.

Find your best picture and insist, 'make me look like this'

How many people have we told to watch

Sweet Movie frosted like a biscuit

Hypersensitive to heat, when we were young the underbrush

Seemed to glow with scattered trash

Quilted mattress propped up on a fallen tree limb

Porn soaked in rain, our bodies fuse together

Into a hunk of pink pulp, a borderless opening

Sucking us through the outskirts of suburban lawns

Strikingly similar to the allure of James and the Giant Peach

When I was young snuggled in bed almost tasting the sticky heat

Queer family of affinity nestled close to the pit

We sold our soul to whatever swarms below the gravel

No, not gravel but a bed of sugar

III.

Steady as a three-legged cauldron

I kiss the ring of The Lesbian Body for Monique Wittig

Who made me reevaluate the preface song could be

Our body a grave for exhumation

Fingers fumbling at the laces of your chest

This whole armor of God so ill fitting

We depend on a rainbow against extinction

The pain and pleasure of confection more complex than you think

There's a limit to our softness we've not yet reached

No a hardness wet and connected

To what could be called the creamy center better yet

An urge to bite down on your cheek

To leave an imprint of my teeth unique as a snowflake

Slick with drool and the memory of baring them

'Choosing a haircut makes this one a girl / or lists to do. You are a girl, one with a hairdo' –Trish Salah

SNAPCHAT DYSMORPHIA

I call us baby and everything is new

Flirting with disaster

Suckling on a tender

Blood to blood marriage that anoints

Us in a bizarre fairy dust

We start not by flying but breathing

Underwater, we're made for adornment

Born with the ideal

Accessories, Cronenberg-esque

Viscera providing border and overflow I choose a face swap

Trading what seems best for a merger

Hoping for the greater good

A dizzy landscape for birds to circle

Getting ready for love

Bopped on the head

By something fuzzy

I want to be eaten in the garden

We want to eat the red curtain

That falls between us

DIABOLIQUE

Asleep our reflection appears smeared

We wear a shade called underage coven

This imagined abundance of heresy

We're training ourselves

To draw a line with our eyes closed

To disappear completely

WESTERN MYTHOLOGY
For Joseph Bradshaw

I will be a false glue, made for you

Rick Owens, R.A.M.O.N.E.S, A$AP

'Dizzy as the green of currency'

I will be Jennifer Lopez in the cell, 'his mind is her prison'

When I was young we wanted 'My Buddy and Me'

Still scared of the thought

A doll could come alive we sleep in the basement beside

A curio cabinet filled with porcelain figurines

Whose paleness compressed to blush is so uncanny

What makes one an American Girl

Is a song to sing on a road to nowhere

The petty security of this vintage, how it will hold you so tight

It's cutting off the blood flow

Can we blush and be comfortable at the same time?

A theory for nascent dread and impulse shopping

Faux haute couture, gore modeled in four dimensions

'The hoax of memory,' the hoax of daddy

What pictures do you see in the smoke that comes out of me —Dia Felix

TOWER OF BABEL

We listen to Slow Wine Mixtape and read The Countersexual
    Manifesto

A reading group is planned in the sense that some friends become
    coconspirators

In the sense that there's a basic misunderstanding of what we might
    imagine on our own

'A shifting I chases a shifting you'

Not exactly true but it sounds right in this moment when we're all
    speaking at the same time

I fall in love with our friends and it seems dangerous without clear
    definition

Our very best intentions meet at oblique angles, flip then bounce

Working it hard I worry a lot about being misunderstood and lose
    control of my words

Say "friend," say "love"

I want to say 'some things last a long time' devoid of any bloodthirsty intimacy

I feel Gucci guilty

Too easily my inflection slips upward into universals

I'm trying my best to age without concession so the conversation twists
    into what if

Our doom is a necessity like how you think about suffering

Being a collection of eroding holes in constant need of attention

And how do you love after God, blah...blah...blah, I'm feeling myself
disappear

In the first story that comes to mind I am a crone hiding in the bushes

Next to the tower waiting to catch the secret lovers in the act

Waiting for the right words in the right order I lick my lips

I'm endlessly spurned but ready, I've never been this close to quote
unquote romance before

I put the book spine straight on my lap like a cartoon tent

You put your finger in my nose, you're looking for my spirit

PURPLE PROSE

Royal we, as in guillotine

A single tear on our cheek

Sincerity, love, or a puck of tar

Flattened by pressure

Our love is a machine

Plowing through a landscape of cocks

Pop punk, pink and black

Blazed by a mall fountain

Lost in a cloud of lush

Our dilettantish nostalgia

Relying on the constant in and out

The day to day

A cosmic fuck machine

An in and out

So regular we could almost fall sleep

NATURE VS NATURE

I first saw my horizon end beneath the foothills of Boulder

Exuberant sky unable to hold the rain, each afternoon is a cafe

I read Wrong

And watch the tiny arc of a puckering asshole form its own
microclimate

We worshiped a faith of inversion

These dizzying heights feel super religious

Each day a storm that fizzles into crystalline detail

Our stubborn look frozen by a coat of chemical spray

Clump of hair stiff as agave

Nihil of endless abundance

Stretching I press my frock between earth and heaven

Our body invents warmth

I read Cunt Ups on the edge of a fire pit

In a land of perpetually unhealthy air

Lungs like flat spinnarets of cotton candy

Listen to Fields of Rhye and my heart disintegrates

Wake up sucking on a bowl like an unwashed toe

Giddy as an empty shirt

That billows my torso into an aerie outline

I was a fire break, a pergola, a technicolor cairn

The biggest selfie attraction the desert has to offer

A queen-sized comforter tossed over the Sierras at dusk

There's a flimsy string that says Do Not Cross

And I can't escape this border of self mythologizing

But I want the poise of what's forbidden, its deceptive stillness

Our throat a slab of rock in Death Valley

Your touch, a sudden cloudburst

WYRM MOON

A droopy queen

A globular tomb

Petite destroyer

A chaste crust

A sugar cube

Dripping white sap

Pink jelly

Full of hell

A vernal grub

A vernal grub

A vernal grub

Daughter of all

MYCELIUM

For Lindsey Boldt

If I had a wand I would put curls in my hair

Stir two tablespoons of epsom salt in this drink

I read your article, I think we're both

On a rocky bluff craving hydration

Slimed in sunscreen beneath brilliant diversions

They say seeing is believing

On our backs we're light as a feather

Buoyed above the canopy of a kelp forest

I couldn't transcend the cloying

Gentle touch of a florist's memento mori

The tumultuous love affair between oil and water

Original packaging, thick prismatic sheen

A million years asleep in a glass coffin

When we're finally in the ground we'll share everything

CONCEPTUAL ROMANCE

All our friends walk with the dead

In sunhats and maxi-dresses

Band tees and bandeaus, acrylic

Necessities of faith in this material world

I will bury my thoughts

Like the one ring deep in a pile of delicates

Blouson stinking like rot

I will shave my head, drape a lace mantle

Like a second skin, a mask, a pathogen

A sad song named "Demi Moore"

Overripe, a skull dripping with pearls

Ears filled with dirt

The queen of the underworld sighing

In my mind thick as mohair

FUCK MACHINES

I lick the edge of your glass to claim what's left behind

I hate the word tender, maybe our lack

Where pushback feels taxing, less urgent, Dionysian

Tinsel will burn if you try hard enough

At the coven we're introduced to a film

Where two siblings share the same body

Like Evolution the film there's an insistence on no time

For lubricant the bug up his ass needed to be removed

Or a rib or his balls, something immediately accessible

Stuck inside a moment of horror, a joke

Where the alien invasion is a sex machine I'm tender

Where tinsel is snow without need for coldness

Where pulp is an added bonus and an insult

My progress versus our pleasure

And honey, the sweetest noise on Earth

SUPERSYMMETRY

The fruit bowl is empty so we sleep in

The retrograde glow of one's friends-to-be

I teased a wet dream about a universe

That oscillates so no worries about completion

I was mad at the certainty, the Big Bang

Baroque hunting scenes, the idea of being Rubenesque

Blushing all over, a soft swollen repose

The object of this voyeur whose gaze had strayed

For a moment we thought it lovely as an arrangement of produce

Ham, jonquils, heavy scrotum of hosiery and pearls

The romance of mishearing

'Kiss a sunset pink,' non-toxic manicure

Julian suggests 'a cricket on a heap of trash'

SEX MACHINES

Laura writes of realism as verisimilitude in drag

We're talking about the terror of beauty

Tracing the edges of the empty space in your

Self-satisfied pleasure curling into resistance

Let's Play Tag Online

'The clouds molest me in the baroque dark'

The sexiness of an indentation

Which seems like a history we can trust

What's terrible about this look?

Resigned to a digital gallery we just swipe through

A sparse no man's land where the air is drowned in lotion

Metallic water streaming down a plastic curtain

Something hard falling out of something soft

The idea of hitting bottom just an abstraction, a fossil liquid, a taxonomy

So much lotion it's all feeling

Like a spongy dessert

When scale is discarded our profile becomes landscape

And I am the hole where the Lord is born

An oubliette, compact and black as a bible

Receptivity is a blessing from the outside

I was asked what I wanted to be when I grew up

I said a farmer's daughter

Knotted flannel tossed across

A blood red barn door, tiny cutoffs

Melting into the decor, all denim and ponytails

More than corn fed

The culmination of your basest fantasy

The world had ended and we hadn't noticed

In high school I was a melancholic cowhand

The bad romance of Scott Walker's Black Sheep Boy

I knew something heavenly was coming

A sickly funnel spinning above our bed

This green expanse is not a sign of health, but

A myth born of the need to compare pleasures

I was naked in the water, I was living eons beneath a dune

It was night, I was licking frosting off a beater

I was slime evolving, I was acid, bacteria growing inside a blossom

I was fluff and fluffing, dust floating upward into a bank of klieg lights

I was the umbilical cord that circulated your blood

We color our hair and the spectrum thickens

ADAM AND EVE

I ask god to drop a pearl in my mouth

It's the least they can do

I worry about being inscrutable

                         Not unbeautiful

A metaphysics, a shaky equilibrium

I circle the drain in cool water

The sewer makes a claim I can't dispute

Indulgent we expand this vanishing point

A velour couch that can swallows us whole

                  If I could I would

Drink a bubble tea every day

Cut off my nose despite our face

And in its place grow

A flower that smells like desecration

It was meant to sweeten and wither

How do you know where the sky starts. / perhaps it is touching your skin – Francesca Lisette

MERKIN

Bottomless I flop in the pool

Turn sunshine to chlorine green like a dying star

Stoya says 'On a pedestal in a garbage can'

Form is infinity broken

At 38 I'm completely transparent

Mortified by my barest fantasy

Fuck infinity, you're as old as you feel

My sex floated above oceans before they receded

I saw the earth buckle, transform

A mountainside emerge from unbearable pressure

I reached down to hold my chest, invisible

Full of heat and insolvency, dry as a bone

Every day junk arrives in the mail

It could be anyone it's addressed to

Picture my name like the partition between two restrooms

This fountain won't hold its weight

I'm topheavy, my mind is overflowing

My ass unyielding, nothing like a morality play

To associate this feeling of needing more skin

I took the stud out, there's still a hole in my tongue

*

I place an ad with my look

Soft butch seeking hard femme

I wanted more than I knew

I felt the impulse sucking me in

I bought a bralette at Gap Body

Its tenderness was rough on the hottest day of the year

The meadow where everything grows according to its own something

I wanted to find myself in a history of the occult

Fashion, the witch's greatest friend

*

Pale and skinny as tapeworms

Ever resistant to the effects of the California sun

We can all go fuck ourselves

And thus unsexed be reborn

I steal a bodysuit at Aerie

There're limits to what we understand

SPIT ON YOUR GRAVE

There's a bruise above both eyes

Luxury queen smirking on the chopping block

Valerie and her week of wonders

Soft lighting and gossamer sheets

There's a lip bleeding for your fantasy

Cream we washed in pulled from a tit

There's the impression of a hand

Furious with desire and strident

Not bashful, meek or wilting

On the cheek I ripped off the dream

Spent two stacks on a makeup bag

The gore we splashed around in

Demure morse code for personal space

I don't even need this skin

A barb, a knife, an exfoliating scrub

There's a base coat smeared everywhere

Dripping pestilence and honeyed bile

Our smize a black Cheshire cat

A fluffer drowning the room in red

There's pus along the nail-bed a French tip

Agony aunt, inspiration and soul twin

A cleanser applied at night

To sleep with this plan of waking to a new face

I am what I am

The cut, the bruise, spitting up scum

LOVE IS OVERTAKING ME

We live in the buzz of sanguine vinyl

Speaking for itself

All is mostly echo

Sufjan in a Gucci tuxedo

The mystery of love

Where the sentiment disintegrates

You leaned against the inside looking out

I thought the outfit apropos, urban cowboy

Organic sextoy, a theatrical self

Still somewhat romantic, I close my eyes

You whisper and we became a shared secret

Cruelty free, a line dancing thru

Our flannel sheets rearranging the weather

Patrick Haggerty, outlaw lavender

Adrift thinking "portrait" not "port in a storm"

Pink means 'nobody deserves happiness'

I read blood and tears

Weigh creature comforts against

'Goodbye old paint'

A velvet rope unraveling at both ends

A vernacular music

Our foolish fascination fading

Laying steak against a bruise

SKY TRAIL

for Jacob Kahn and Karin Dahl

Dinner, vest and a tent

I read the subject line

In the quiet way friends have to get you up and moving

Beyond what we want to believe

There's water left

In spring, wind off the Pacific seems more real

Clouds mark it and shift the dull white cosmology

Learning their proper names when we were young

We spent the weekend reading to ourselves

Autocorrected to "purses"

All thumbs or schizophrenic screen

Is breeze really a femme sound?

SAILING WITH THE STONE

In this film where chaos reigns

Peahens cry like mountain lions

The sun only sets on the righteous

*

A natural born survivor, Aileen Wuornos

In love with Natalie Merchant's tigerlily

Chose Carnival for her execution song

*

Our makeup is appropriate for the occasion

It comes from dirt, big mothership

I'm sailing with the stone

*

Struggling in an attempt for precision

With a bedazzled knife

We cut through the flimsy packaging

*

'Behind every great man' is

Sephora misinterpreted

Pennywise, not a beautiful wife

HELL PATROL

I've never watched The Exorcist

Yet trying to unmarry me as

With most hallucinations

It's the thought that really counts

*

'On the eve of the apocalypse

The air choked with horsehair'

The plug being pulled

The little sound that I love

*

Blood is spiritual currency

Though I worry about the glamour

A shower for your ass, lying

Facedown in the fountain of youth

*

I'd call it truth, though

More than half the time

I can't hear

What we're saying

SMOKE MACHINE

We get changed in a time machine

A carousel of lowered expectations

Press our face against a flower with no smell

There has to be a reason we breathe

BOTOX

We live as if proper names

Could find cosmetic equivalencies

Supersymmetry is a bogus makeup, yes

The word is gigantic, some would say

Hard to miss, bustling and productive

The metropolitan look

This year's concept album

A block of sullen minimalism

In praise of a manicured idleness

Overclaiming the soft snow

White slumber of dead stars

We kiss and skip over the moon

Its perpetual resurrection is a fairness

Applied liberally in the looking glass

The definition cuts both ways

Heaven is hell squared

A sweetie given a lot of space

I have to make explicit

Implications about what we're doing

Unaware we push the blush away

To expression's edge and over it

The mottled proof our embarrassment

It only looks like we didn't try

When we pinch with a little je ne sais quoi

We're told, 'Ladies pinch'

Crushing the skin w/o remorse

I say 'do we bleed' rhetorically

I wonder, really do we?

FLOURISH

'I created myself to death'

I barely waited for an opening

To speak though I couldn't really say that

You said anything at all

We ignore the history of representation

Verities, forget-me-nots

Some great abstract secret

Defiantly dependent on this crush

Nervous precursor to a glow paint party

Where the anticipation of a sudden drop is killing me

We wriggle into the fire

Wallflowers to this Apollonian morning

Exhausted, tan and downtrodden

Petals unfolding like a reconstructed sweater

This torso of two impossible animals in heat

Venus always works without a net

Using color as a modifier the meek will inherit

The shit of god, the drought of promise

MODELS

We disappear like the eyes of a black cat

In the back of a closet

Scratching at tapestry or crumbled crystal gravel

Contamination is beauty's north star

Whose glow will pass too quickly

In an abstract grand scheme

Death is our little secret

Our applause and fairy dust all used up

I fade out to where opulence is born

A loner in blue mascara

Fingers spread apart by cotton batting

Touching doesn't have to be intimate

With all of us somewhere on the spectrum

Imagine each color holds

A special meaning that can't be translated

Oil stain or northern lights

Visible to those who tend to agree

We blush as a presentiment

We hold it in our pocket

Apply in the rearview

Casually choosing embarrassment

To get us through the day

Circles are gay

We run into foam

SYMBOLISM

The sun swooped in like a hawk from out of the blue

I was adopted as a pet project

She says 'It takes a lot to be someone else but we manage'

Horror demonstrates the pleasure of repetition

*

When Frank was inside his straight BFF

They stared at the sun hovering like a ghost above the dunes

Decades later on another coast

I was searching for the sky, head in the sand

Basking on one leg, turning pink

In the distance where water falls off the edge of the earth

I hear mermaids calling to me

Scales glinting like the display case at Claire's

Like a rainbow

Hung in a window

I feel guilty for being this way

Sundrenched and melancholy

The type of poet who eats the sun and writes about it

In the moonlight where the only beauty is reflection

Their gender roles on spin cycle

*

Femme fatale bent

Imperious over a drink

Dripping with sherbet

Sweating, God calls "not it!"

We linger at the ocean

To pretend your interest still exists

The separation between

Water and sky disappears

Basic Instinct

Verses Fatal Attraction

Cold blood under the mask of

Domestic bliss

What the California coastline engenders

A sunset dramatic enough

To transform a stock image

Into last call

'Sun, meet the end of all our days'

*

This roast is tender and seasoned to perfection

The sun just hangs off my shoulder

I have a lot of feelings for you

Sending hugs and kisses from paradise

I WANTED TO SAY FOREVER

I'm lounging where imagination ends

Trying to come to terms with a moment

That slides into banality, but wait

I want to be clear, understood

We get a makeover like it's the first morning

Of the new year in a bed

At the edge of something unexplored

This feeling of falling short always here

Never more apparent, the veneer of afterglow

Where celebration equals crying to Aretha Franklin

To predict an endless replay of loss

To be what I wanted to say, forever

So close our navigation leans towards the future perfect

Trembling a little like tonight's hard wind through frosted tips

A music that wants to burrow inside our chest

Imagine what it looks like talking to myself

The holidays are over, we lean toward their allure

Sparkle and Fade

I wanted you to love me back and forth

We spend most of our time singing in the dark

SLIPKNOT

At our barest we hold close to

The subliminal, how singular details begin

To overlap, indistinct scatter at first

Sunlight through black lace

All angles below a sheet

Where seduction ripens, bloom

Blush and droplet, hard rubber

Pistil, watery strings then sophoric dust

A floral rudder turning in the dark

Nightie heaped at the doorstep

oncession to the pull of

The sun we guess impatient for

Delicious shadow

And sound without origin

We were hoping tomorrow would

Never come and it didn't yet

Our nails chipped regardless we felt

A plastic blossom somewhat

Delicate and mostly unnecessary

Earnest, wooden hard femme

Dragged towards the source

Cotton, lipstick, Vaseline

The aesthetics of disappearance

Untended, a nest of violent rays

Baby's face mistaken for a moon

Bleached tattoo, just barely held together

In a silk confection that hosts

This bouquet of poor forgeries

The barest feeling we curve into

A brace or a velvet string, fishnets

Strung out between world

So then one may sketch her spending her morning in a China robe of ambiguous gender among her books – Virginia Woolf

MAGIC MOUNTAIN

Impossibly pretty day, now that we've agreed to become the same person

Midway to your memorial

On the Bay Bridge listening to Saltarello by Dead Can Dance

Then Rights for Gays, hey moon, we all met in the middle of a meadow

Summer of Love part two, in the middle of the hardest year since I can't remember when

Why does it take the death of someone we love to press into our hands

A book that could've saved our own past lives

Just some luck, I guess, I wish I'd read The Left Hand of Darkness before I curled up in a bus headed north

In the middle of a storm that spelled disaster with four letters and a question mark,

Or when I used to play Homogenic in bed, imagining myself inside the song

'I'm a fountain of blood, in the shape of a girl'

In retrospect, I realize I'm lucky

I found Margery Kempe when I was still young enough to crush hard and dissolve

Jesus my distant lover, now and forever ever, "Love" or

"Luck," they seem like such insufficient words

All these songs from a housewarming playlist set on random

I love your story of getting fucked in a copy machine, Impossible Princess

It makes me think of that perfect gothy tableau in Margery

Bob and his soon-to-be ex standing beside a frozen waterfall

Watching some unnamed river slide behind a hole in the ice

I can almost see the heat of their breathing rise off the page like a
    manifestation of some inner departure

And Steve's Elegy too, 'the dead communicate with us in strange ways'

Its funny the impermanence of all that's fleeting, I welcomed it inside me

And watched a pink petal fall from a centerpiece on the dais

During one of the eulogies—this is not an image for effect

It really happened—like the hush of a bird alighting on a podium

Ariana writes about the communal ecstasy Bernie's bird and Mozart's Requiem

In A Sand Book then later titles a section 'the saddest year of my life,'
    which feels abundant and yes

To be honest a little melodramatic

Though apropos as well, 'there is honey in the groin,' I imagine

Julian's "writing feeling" which for me starts at the bottom of my prostate

A polka dot of warm pressure tugging me backward

And a sudden rush of goosebumps, giving the skin of my ass some rouche

This persistent sense of déjà vu

I lose focus when I read

Shy, I Cry Like a Baby

Diary of a Teenage Girl

Pink Steam, Close to the Knives, so many readings this weekend

Birthdays at Land's End, the northern tier of

The Golden Gate emerging from clouds

Like a smoke ring on the edge of collapse

I was flipping through Punk Rock is Cool for the End of the World

Looking for somewhere solid to land

Sandblown and battered at Baker Beach

Tumbled again and again by the waves

Stubborn, I refused to yield an inch of belabored joy

'The intimations of cancer'

Francesca's Crying in the Sun

I lied and told Connie growing up in the church taught me how to read closely

Like I wasn't already exhausted every Sunday morning

Struggling to feel the touch of the spirit

But I remember I was in tears the first time

I read I Remember, Mausoleum of Lovers, Rumored Place

Or palace, California Dreamin sometimes I think you taught me how to lie sweetly

Jesus God Almighty, oh my sweet lord

Meet me at the bottom of the swimming pool

I sit with things dying, you sit with things reborn

'Nobody wants a lonely heart,' an occasional poem, song or bon mot

Like 'wherever you go, there you are,' 'islands in the stream'

And 'just like heaven,' I'm running out of time

CALL HER GREEN

Drunk in a pile of rosebuds

Honeyed lovers, hive-minded

Asleep on the wing, confused as me

Space is disappearing and you my singularity

It's evening, it's morning

Average star I feel your breeze

ACKNOWLEDGEMENTS

Thank you to Sara Larsen, Laura Woltag, Nick DeBoer, Joseph Bradshaw, Lauren Levin, Jacob Kahn, and Lindsey Boldt for reading early versions of this book and offering extremely helpful thoughts and suggestions.

Many thanks and hearts to Julian Talamantez Brolaski, Laura Moriarty, and Vi Khi Nao for their kind words. Thank you to the speCt! team for their thoughtfulness and support.

Thank you most of all to Ivy, my first and best reader.

Earlier versions of some of these poems have appeared in *Mirage #5*/Period(ical), *Social Text*, *Dusie*, *Baest*, *Bedfellows*, *Tammy*, *Splinter*, *Ramblr*, *Bodega*, *Metatron*, the tiny, *Fetch*, *G U E S T*, and *We Want it All: An Anthology of Radical Trans Poetics* (Nightboat, 2020).

A selection of these poems was published as a chapbook by b l u s h in 2019.

JAMIE TOWNSEND is a genderqueer poet and editor living in Oakland. They are the author of 6 chapbooks as well as the long-form collection *Shade* (Elis Press, 2015). They are also the editor of *Beautiful Aliens: A Steve Abbott Reader* (Nightboat, 2019) and *Libertines in the Ante-Room of Love: Poets on Punk* (Jet Tone, 2019). With Nick DeBoer they curate *Elderly*.

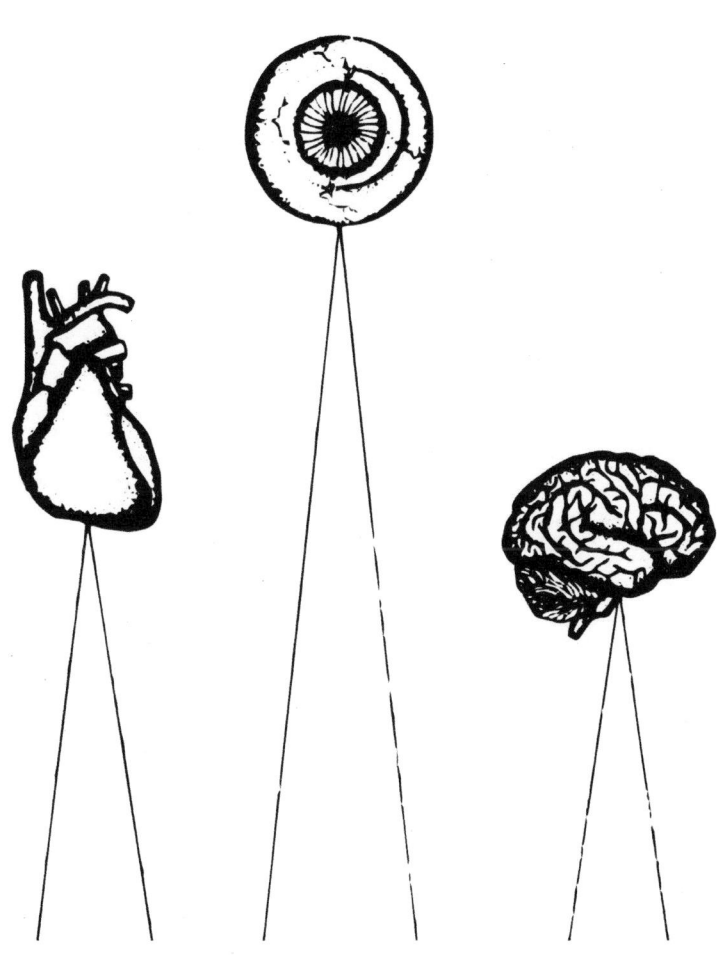